metamorphoses
(after Ovid)

Gari Jones

Published by Playdead Press 2013

© Gari Jones 2013

Gari Jones has asserted his rights under the Copyright, Design and Patents Act, 1988, to be identified as the author of this work.

A CIP catalogue record for this book is available from the British Library.

ISBN 978-0-9576792-8-3

Caution
All rights whatsoever in this play are strictly reserved and application for performance should be sought through the author before rehearsals begin. No performance may be given unless a license has been obtained.

This book is sold subject to the condition that it shall not by way of trade or otherwise, be lent, resold, hired out, or otherwise circulated without the publisher's prior consent in any form of binding or cover other than that in which it is published and without a similar condition including this condition being imposed on the subsequent purchaser.

Printed by BPUK

Playdead Press
www.playdeadpress.com

Gari Jones is an established and experienced Director and Writer. With over twenty years experience, his work has been seen at the Royal National Theatre, the Almeida, the Old Vic, the Young Vic, in the West End, on Broadway, in squat venues, churches, car-parks, night clubs, warehouses and has also toured extensively throughout the UK and internationally, as well as in many other Theatres and Drama Schools. He has devised, worked with writers on new plays, directed contemporary and classical work, and created a range of site-specific, multi-media & cross-art work.

This book is dedicated to my amazing wife and children,
without whom I would have lost all hope.

First performed at the Mercury Theatre, Colchester, produced by renegade in collaboration with Lakeside Theatre on 11th September 2013

One   Pandora/Mum/Echo/Pomona/Hunger/Hypnos
Performed by Abi Bing

Two   Aglauros/Eurydice/Morpheus
Performed by Emily Dixon

Three Thisbe/Alcyone
Performed by Sophie Mitchell

Four   Lycaon/Narcissus/Vertumnus/Envy
Performed by Dan Shambrook

Five   Phaeton/Orpheus
Performed by Richard Hornsby

Six   Phoebus/Pyramus/Midas/Pygmalion
Performed by Mike Prokopiou

Director	Gari Jones
Sound Designer	Marcus Christensen
Lighting Designer	David Digby
Stage Manager	Lucy Quinton
Movement Director	Dan Shambrook
Production Assistant	Faye-Justine Watson

With thanks to Churches Conservation Trust, Lakeside Theatre, Mercury Theatre, Colchester Arts Centre, Slackspace, Cram Design, My Icon, Harry Harris, Barbara Peirson, Genine Sumner, Amanda Jones.

This work is part of renegade, existing to showcase artists and work in all mediums, to provide opportunity, to collaborate and to create innovative work and events. A new way of thinking. A needs must. A sign of the times. An invitation to be heard. Voices In The Dark. Fragments Rise Like Moths From The Dust.

@renegade pariah
www.facebook.com/fragmentsinthedust

Note: There should be a constant sense of a group of storytellers and the text should always be played as new and spontaneous. Additions can be made to the text which allow the actors to comment when and where appropriate on how something is played or said. It's a simple but effective device to continually create a sense of improvisation and storytelling. However believably and truthfully something is played, the actor can easily switch to narrative again. Each storyteller, no matter how many 'parts' are assigned, essentially has one through story to tell and changes are part of the lesson and discovery within their story. Minimal set is required. We used a box which housed water, with an additional two boxes from which to pull props and costume additions. We also used a rostra area at one end. Sound and light can be used to enhance atmosphere and to help aid ambience, time, location and so on.

A Cast of Six:

One	Pandora/ Mum/ Echo/ Pomona/ Hunger/ Hypnos
Two	Aglauros (*Aglooros*)/ Eurydice (*Yuridisee*)/ Morpheus
Three	Thisbe/ Alcyone (*Alsee-aney (as in a key*)
Four	Lycaon (Lie-con)/ Narcissus/ Vertumnus/ Envy
Five	Phaethon (*fayten (as in satan*)/ Orpheus
Six	Phoebus/ Pyramus/ Midas/ Pygmalion

Stories included in part: The Creation/ The Four Ages/ Lycaon/Pandora/ Phaethon & Phoebus/ Aglauros' Envy/ Pyramus & Thisbe/ Narcissus & Echo/ Vertumnus & Pomona/ Orpheus & Eurydice/ Alcyone & Ceyx/ Erysichton/ Midas/ Pygmalion/

Six   Bodies, I have in mind, and how they can change to assume new shapes...

Metamorphosis, its plural metamorpho-ses... transformation... a term used to describe a form of development, a change. Whether profound and complete, whether from one stage to the next in life history, a change in form or appearance, or structure, a change in character, condition, function, circumstance, a type of alteration or degeneration in which there is tissue change...

Three   (*Cuts in*) Transfiguration: the metamorphosis of the old house into something new and exciting...

Four   (*Cuts in*) It is often the biological process by which an animal develops, a degenerative pathological change in the structure of a particular body tissue, involving a conspicuous and relatively abrupt change in form or structure through cell growth or differentiation...

One   Insects, amphibians, molluscs, crustaceans, many of them undergo metamorphosis, sometimes also involving a change in habitat, water to land for example...

Five   Some go through many stages, starting with the larva or nymph stage, sometimes then to pupa, on to adult...

Two   And time has a huge part to play, changing its mind from one species to another; the mayfly, the non-eating adult lives for just one day…

Four   The cicada, whose juvenile stage remains underground for up to 17 years…

Three   The housefly: Egg, one day, Larva, two weeks, Pupa, one week, Adult, two weeks…

Six   And the Cockroach: Egg, one month, Larva, three months, there is no pupa stage. Adult. Nine months.

Ring any bells?

(*Women take over*)

One   And what causes these changes, these metamorphoses? Nature. Sure science, biology, emotion, but essentially, nature.

Three   The grass and the dirt we walk on, the sky we stand beneath, whether it glows with the moon or gleams with the sun.

(*Women look at the Men*)

Two   And within that, the complexities, perhaps the simplicities, of every look in every pair of eyes when they meet for the very first time.

One   And then something extraordinary can happen.

Three   Extra ordinary.

Two   Unexplainable.

(*Pause. Men take over*)

Five   There is chaos in our lives all the time, whether that we witness in others...

Four   ...that we see on the news...

Six   ...that we feel in ourselves, whether it's someone else's or not.

Four   We still feel a sense of pain, of empathy, of guilt.

Five   We all feel a sense of chaos from time to time.

Six   And it is from that chaos, that sense of despair or loss, of not coping, that we grow, we develop...

Five   We learn.

Four It is from that that life comes, that incredible things start to happen.

(*Pause*)

One It is a womb then, from which everything is born.

Three Initially this chaos was a heap of things just clashing together.

Two A jumble sale of elemental debris.

Six Nothing had found its place.

Four There was no sun

One No moon.

Five Where there was air…

Two There was sea and earth.

Four In the gloom, vague shapes would appear for a moment before giving way.

Six Cold warred with hot.

Three Wet with dry.

One Soft with hard.

Five   Buoyancy with weightlessness.

Two   It just hung.

(*Pause*)

Four   Then there came a tiny spark that started to glow in the dark.

Three   Illuminating the earth.

Six   And thus, the first, slow metamorphosis began.

(*Pause. A harmony starts to infiltrate*)

One   The bluest part split from the rest and suspended itself to form the skies, followed by the air, their lack of weightlessness moving them up.

Five   Next the earth, being heavier, fell below. The land arranged itself, was moulded and sculpted into valleys and mountains...

(*Looking at each other*)

Two   A work of wonder created a harmonious cosmos...

Four   A perfection of nature...

Three   A true work of art...

Six   A new kind of beauty.

(*Pause*)

One   Then came creatures, animals, each with different strengths and Speeds...

Two   One had wings...

Three   Another claws...

One   Fish swam in the sea...

Two   Birds flew in the air...

Three   And beasts roamed the earth.

(*Beat*)

Two   The air was clear and the stars twinkled and shone out.

One   It was like a dream of purity.

(*Beat*)

Three   But it was silent.

Two   There were no words.

(*Pause*)

One A different kind of animal was needed.

Three Some say God created humans from his divine substance.

Two Others maintain that humanity came from the natural order, born out of the earth and the ether and mixed with rainwater.

(*Man is presented*)

One Either way, man arose…

Four Whilst some animals turned their faces down to sniff and look at the Earth…

Six Man stood tall…

Five Looking at the heavens with his head to the stars.

(*Pause*)

Four But man wasn't always as we now perceive. It took time.

Six First came the Golden Age, where everything was fresh and new and, without the compulsion of laws and the fear of punishment, men were decent, fair and generous. Through lifetimes of peace, man lived as one with nature.

Five Then came the Silver Age when man began to learn and develop. From that knowledge, standards grew. But with that came greed. Animals were used and abused to create more. New emotions began to occur as one man looked at another with a darkness in his eye.

Four Last, the Iron Age. And with that, pouring as if from a fire, a river of molten evil. Modesty and truth fled the Earth. Envy, deceit and violence prevailed as man craved more of everything as he unleashed endless possibilities. The Earth was decimated through greed.

Five But as man learnt what was possible, there were other lessons: Understanding, empathy, truth, love.

Lyc. Man was not all good, although who's to say what's good and what's bad. The divide blurs and shifts for everyone, particularly Lycaon. The story goes that he had…

Two (*Cuts in*) Lycanthropy is the ability to transform, to metamorphose into a wolf.

Three Or sometimes to absorb its characteristics, whilst still retaining human form.

Lyc. Lycaon was a man turned wolf.

Six It can also be that it is just the soul that goes forth to destroy, whilst leaving the body in a state of trance.

Five It might be the messenger of the human, a real animal or spirit whose deep connection with its owner means that any injury or damage needs reciprocation.

Two A kind of subliminal revenge, if you like.

Three Yes, or karma... if you like.

Six But remember this: All emotion will reveal itself physically. Whatever is felt will somehow resolve in a physical manifestation of some sort or another.

Five This kind of change finds its origins mingling a...

Six What? Mingling?

Five Yes, mingling... a belief in reincarnation, in the sharing of souls between humans and non-humans.

Two   Spirits.

Six   Yes. And a belief in human ghosts becoming non-human entities after death.

(*Pause*)

Lyc.   The story goes that Lycaon had taken a man in and given him shelter. An act, it would seem, of selflessness and generosity. But Lycaon was neither of these things. Having served his guest his own brother to eat, to prove who this man really was, he went to kill him in the dead of night.

(*Physical battle*)

Five   But the man had been sleeping with one eye open and cursed him, changing him…

Lyc.   He changed. Himself.

Six   Lycanthropy is also a mental illness where the patient has delusions that he has turned into a wolf, is lycanthropic.

Lyc.   There's no delusion.

Six   Clinical lycanthropy.

Lyc. Lycaon saw things differently. And what he saw he didn't like. He was hungry to destroy it, to annihilate it, by whatever means.

(*Pause*)

Two What did man need to find some kind of resolution?

1/2/3 Woman

(*Woman is presented*)

Pand. And so the first woman was created Pandora.

Three 'She to whom all gifts were given.'

Two Beauty.

Three Grace.

Two Poise.

Three A wiggle.

Five To die for.

Six Persuasion.

Three Multi-tasking skills and expertise.

Lyc. A shameful and manipulative mind and a thieving, deceitful nature.

Two The power of speech.

Lyc. Lies.

Three Clever and intelligent words.

Lyc. And a sorrow to men who live on bread.

(*Beat*)

Five She's beautiful.

Six Breathtaking.

Five I didn't believe in Angels. Until now.

(*Beat*)

Three Euphoria. The anterior cingulate is the part of the brain that creates such feelings of happiness.

Two The medial insular is associated with a variety of emotions, but if there are lesions there can be drastic consequences, not least of which relates to the interpretation of visual input.

Three Finally, the putamen…

Two   And caudate…

Three   Nucleus lie deep within the brain and are the more common stimulants to positive emotion.

(*The men have separated and stare at Pandora*)

Lyc.   Who did Lycaon answer to? He was just the messenger.

The illusive figure of man turned wolf despised humanity. It sickened him and he sought to destroy it by whatever means necessary.

(*Pause*)

Five   No. I don't trust this.

(*To Six*) Don't accept her.

Six   Look at her.

Five   I know. But don't accept.

Six   You need to learn to trust a little more.

She's incredible. There is no way that something so beautiful can cause harm or house evil.

Five   Don't say you weren't warned. You mug.

(*Pause. The Man and Woman assess each other and slowly hold hands*)

> Love is a natural weakness bequeathed to us by the first man, linking our present to the roots of the past and the dome of the future.

Two   And as time taught them how to share, to love and to be…

Three   It also taught woman how to use what she had. Only when necessary.

(*Man and Woman together. Pandora should change constantly from sympathy, to lust, to anger, to sad, to stern. The man remains absorbed with his own chain of thought, confused*)

Six   (*To Pandora*) You say you love me for who I am, but who you think I am is not who I am.

Pand.   (*To him*) It's hard for me to be who I am when we're together because I think I have to be who you think I am.

Six   But I don't know exactly who it is you think I am.

Pand.   Nor I you.

Six Who I am is something I recognise when someone tells me who I am not.

Pand. I think that's not who I am.

Six You must really love me.

(*Beat*)

Lyc. Love is a poison injected by vipers from the caverns of hell.

(*The Man and Woman kiss*)

> You can cover it up, call it the honeymoon period, but the cracks will show. And once drunk - intoxicated and destined to die a long, slow, painful death.

(*The Man watches Lycaon place a box*)

Six Come away.

Pand. What's in the box?

Six (*Snaps*) Nothing.

Pand. Darling.

Six Sorry.

Just leave it.

Pand. But I want…

Six I mean it.

Pand. I want to know what's in it.

Six I want doesn't get.

(*Beat*)

Where's this nasty curiosity, this probing coming from?

Pand. I don't know.

Six I don't like it.

Pand. I'm learning. That's all. Every day I am learning.

Six Yes. As am I.

Now come away.

(*Pause*)

I said Come away.

Pand. No.

Six   You're refusing me?

Pand. I am.

(*He leaves. She stares at the box*)

>It's smiling at me.

(*She goes closer*)

>It's speaking to me.

(*He returns*)

Six   Look, I don't want to argue.

Pand. No.

Six   If I say no to you, I will lose you and yet... if I say yes I lose myself.

Pand. Even if you win, you lose.

(*Beat*)

Six   We're still learning, that's all.

Pand. Yes. That's all.

(*He is unsure as to whether to leave her*)

Don't you trust me?

(*He smiles and leaves*)

(*To the box*) Hello?

Yes. Yes.

Lyc. And she did it!

(*She opens the box*)

Lyc. All the diseases, sorrows, vices and crimes of the world flew from the box, nasty winged creatures, pricking and stinging her.

Two Envy.

Five Greed.

Lyc. Vanity.

Three Anger.

Five Revenge.

Two Illness.

Three Hunger.

Lyc.   Until they flew off.

(*Pause*)

Evil had entered the world.

(*Pandora is hurt, but clutches the box*)

Six   What have you done?

(*She slowly opens the box*)

Pand.   Hope.

Six   You hope what exactly?

Pand.   Hope remains.

Look. It's still in there.

Six   Yes. (*Pointed*) It didn't get out.

Pand.   Even when things feel like they can't get any worse, you always have hope.

Lyc.   (*Very sarcastic*) Great. Fantastic.

Woman: beautiful exterior, perhaps even posterior. But inside: worthless and weak. A liar and a thief. A controlling parasite with an unyielding appetite for food and unnecessaries, making him poor. And for sex, making him feeble, whilst slowly winding him around her little finger.

Let the games begin.

(*Starts to go*)

Three So man found woman. But it would only get more complex, more chaotic, as the world was peopled.

(*Hearing this, he can't help himself*)

Lyc. Why? Why do we never learn? The child won't save these fractured relationships and it doesn't deserve to be born into this revolting chasm of war and hatred. How many more will it take? How many more terminations, mistakes, tortured, unloved kids, going through life alone and angry?

(*Pause. All eyes on him*)

Sorry. My issue.

(*Pause*)

Two One of the most amazing metamorphoses is the cycle of pregnancy and birth – the changes in the mother and the child, from that initial twinkle in the eye.

Lyc. Or struggle in a darkened corner.

(*Pandora holds a baby*)

Pand. Shine bright, little one.

Three What are the effects of the trauma of birth? That sense of overwhelming mortal threat, caught in a monstrous claustrophobic nightmare, helplessness, hopelessness...

Two (*Cuts in*) What an incredible mind-blowing change for the child as it starts its tunnelled journey into the unknown.

Six What are we going to call it?

Pand. Phaeton. The shining one.

Two So out it comes. This tiny, helpless, defenceless... innocent? Maybe. Certain, though, is its absolute dependency on it's creators for everything.

Three Including unconditional love. We are all born for love. It's the principle for existence.

Two A sponge, nevertheless, that absorbs literally everything.

Two/Three (*At the baby*) Hello there. Cootchy-coo. Cootchy-coo.

(*They pull scary faces and the baby is quickly moved away*)

Pand. The parent must be careful as to what and indeed who it allows the child to witness. Not everyone is to be trusted.

Three If only they stayed as a baby.

(*Baby becomes Phaeton*)

Pand. If only.

Phaet. Mum!

Pand. Sorry darling.

Two But, no. A further metamorphosis begins its magic.

(*She takes Phaeton's hand*)

Three Nature takes one hand…

(*Pandora takes the other*)

Two …nurture grabs the other and then the tug-of-war begins.

(*A face off. A struggle*)

Three   But the day will always come when we have to let go.

Pand.   I don't want to.

Two   Love is the child of illusion.

Three   And the parent of disillusion.

(*They let Phaeton go and watch as he joins his 'friends'*)

Two   (*Looking at the kids*) The children of men and women are the flowers of love and compassion.

Three   The flowers are the children of nature... and of the Sun.

(*Beat*)

Four   (*Laughs*) The Sun?

That, Phaethon, makes you a flower.

Six   A Pansy.

Four   And your Dad... is a leech.

Phaet.   No he's not.

Six   He's a maggot.

Four   That needs exterminating.

Phaet.   He is not.

Four   And your Mum…

(*He stops and glares*)

Phaet.   Don't you dare.

Four   Your Mum is a liar.

(*He lashes out, goes berserk with rage. It comes to an end*)

Who would believe their dad is the sun.

(*They go, leaving Phaethon alone*)

Phaet.   The sweetest call: mother. Unconditionally moulded in hope and love and all that is pure. She is everything: Consolation when we're sad, help when we're distressed, strength when we're weak. The only real source of tenderness, compassion and forgiveness. If you lose your mother, there's nowhere else to lay your head.

(*Mum is reading the girls' palms*)

Thisbe (*To Phaethon*) What's wrong?

Phaet. Nothing.

Agla. What's wrong with him?

Phaet. I said nothing.

Thisbe Mum, what's wrong with Phaethon?

Mum What is wrong with Phaethon?

(*She goes to him playfully but he moves away*)

What's wrong?

Agla. If you're so depressed why don't you just kill yourself.

Phaet. I just might.

Mum (*To Aglauros*) Be Quiet.

(*To Phaethon*) You wouldn't, would you?

Phaet. Mum, I don't want to talk about it.

Mum How can I help if you don't tell me?

Phaet. You'll only make it worse, because it's your fault.

Mum   What is?

Phaet.   That I haven't got a dad.

(*Beat*)

Mum   You have.

(*Pause*)

Thisbe   (*At Phaeton*) I hate you. I wish you were dead.

Mum   Thisbe.

(*Thisbe goes. Aglauros follows*)

Phaet.   Are you proud of yourself? Are you?

Mum   I've done my best.

Phaet.   Well you should raise your standards.

(*Pause*)

Mum   Have people been teasing you again?

Phaet.   You've got no idea. I can't even answer them. They say horrific things... and I can't say anything. I can't defend him. It's killing me, Mum.

(*Beat*)

    You've done this.

Mum But I've told you.

    I've told you. I don't know what else to say.

Phaet. That's convenient.

Mum I promise you, Phaethon, with all that I am... by this shining orb, which sees and hears me speak, I swear to you that you are the child of the sun, the same sun that guides, lights and heals the world. And if my words are false, may he deny himself to my sight and may the light of this day be the last I ever see.

(*Focuses on Phoebus*)

    I miss him. I miss him so much. I stand and feel him go by every day. Our love isn't gazing at each other, but looking together in the same direction. He washes over me, holding me, with light and warmth.

    But I... I miss him.

(*Pause*)

Phaet. I'm sorry.

(*Pause*)

Why isn't he here though, with us?

Mum Marriage is three parts love and seven parts forgiveness.

(*Pause*)

I knew this day would come at some point.

You should go to him. Talk to him.

Phaet. Really?

(*Transition. Phaethon hugs and leaves his mother as Phoebus and Friends assemble*)

Phoe. Phoebus waited in his lofty hall, polished like fire, buffed to high sheen. Surrounding him were his precious friends and attendants:

Two Day and Month.

Four Year and Century.

Three The seasons. Spring and Summer and Autumn and…

One   And the very overworked Hours, minutes and seconds.

(*Phaethon covers his eyes*)

Phoe.   It's wonderful to see you.

Phaet.   I can barely see you.

(*He is given sunglasses*)

 I want... I want to know if you're really my Dad.

(*Beat*)

 I need to know.

Phoe.   Sorry.

Phaet.   I must know.

Phoe.   Sorry.

(*Pause*)

Phaet.   You're not, are you?

(*Beat*)

 Yes or No? Yes or No?

Phoe.   Yes. Yes, absolutely yes.

Phaet.   Really?

Phoe.   Really.

   I'm sorry I haven't been there. I haven't been around for you, but...

Phaet.   Prove it.

Phoe.   What?

Phaet.   Prove it.

Phoe.   Okay. Whatever you want, whatever you need, it's yours.

Phaet.   Anything?

Phoe.   Yes, anything.

(*Pause*)

Phaet.   Your car. Your sun chariot.

(*Beat*)

   To drive it.

Phoe. When I said anything...

Phaet. For one day.

Phoe. It's too dangerous.

Phaet. You promised.

Phoe. Anything but that.

Phaet. You're not even a man of your word. You're just the same as my so-called mother. But of course, you don't know her, do you?

Phoe. I can't let you.

Phaet. Do you?

Phoe. I love your mother more than you'll ever know.

(*Beat*)

    No one but me has the mettle to handle it. Everything is against you, moving, too quickly. It's chaos. You don't have the skill or the strength to keep it in control.

    Please, something else. Consider the words of a loving father...

Phaet. You're not my Dad.

Phoe. If I'm not, why would I speak with a parents love and concern? You asked me for proof that you're mine. What more do you need than my fear for you. I wish you could see inside me, at my breaking heart. If anything were to happen I couldn't forgive myself. You ask for a fatal gift and yet the world is out there for the taking.

Phaet. I am taking the world.

(*Sarcastic*) Aren't you proud of me? Your son?

Phoe. It is not honour but destruction you seek. Why are you so angry?

Phaet. How dare you have to ask me that?

Four Excuse me, Sir.

Phoe. What is it?

Four The stars and the Moon are withdrawing. It's time.

Phoe. Thank you.

(*Pause*)

Phoe. Don't go too high or you will burn. Nor too low or you will set the Earth on fire.

(*Beat*)

Look, you don't have to do this. Take my love instead. Let me do what I do every day, bringing light and warmth to you, to your mother.

If you will not take my advice, then at least take care. I leave you to chance, which I hope will plan better for you than you have done for yourself.

Phaet. Thank you.

(*Pause*)

The boundless plain of the Universe lay out before him.

Two He sped forward…

Four Cleaving the clouds

Phoe. Outrunning the morning breeze.

One A plaything of physics slightest impulse.

Three As the power of the machine overtook him

Phaet. So too did fear.

Two The constellations scatter

Four The serpent writhes into life.

Phaet. His knees are weak and all he can see is a huge dazzling wrongness and regret.

Three Faster and faster

One Hotter and hotter

Phaet. He wished he'd never questioned his parents.

Phoe. Showering sparks

One The earth bursts into flames

Two Consuming everything

Three Nations flashing

Four Then gone.

Phoe. Unbearable heat.

Phaet. Smoke…

One Shredding his lungs.

Phoe. Heaven transformed into Hell.

One And darkness enveloped him.

(*Pause*)

Phaet. Yes, I regretted it. But once I'd said it I didn't dare take it back. Pride. A damaging commodity. I was angry.

(*Pause*)

Agla. Everyone, the world over, watched the first falling star.

Phoe. The father, stricken, overflowing with grief and regret, covered his face and wept.

Mum (*At Phoebus*) What have you done?

Phoe. For an entire day the Sun didn't appear and the only light was from the embers of the burning earth, sunk into a dreadful dreamscape.

Mum The mother, mute with woe, searched the whole world, until she finally came across her son's body and was able to find some peace.

Agla. His sisters gathered where he lay.

Thisbe And stood in silence.

Agla. Time passed.

Thisbe The moon passed over the sun time and time again.

(*Silence*)

Thisbe I want to go to him. (*She makes to move*) But I can't move.

Agla. I'll help you. (*She makes to move*) I can't move my feet.

Roots hold me.

Thisbe My hair has become leaves.

Agla. My arms are branches.

Thisbe My skin is like bark. It's taking me over.

Both (*Calling*) Mum!

(*In a panic, Mum runs between them kissing them*)

Mum Don't you leave... Don't you leave me too.

(*She tries to tear their bodies from the trees*)

Agla. It hurts. It hurts Mum.

Thisbe Don't... Don't Mum.

(*Pause*)

It'll be alright.

Agla. Bark closed over their mouths leaving a silent loss hanging in the air.

Thisbe Tears still fell and hardened to amber, becoming jewels and ornaments for brides, in the throws of first love.

(*Statues of Thisbe, Aglauros, Mother and Phaethon. Through the following they change*)

Phoe. Phoebus, despising himself and in deep mourning, in time, manages to get back into the cart and assess the damage.

In time the sun replenishes the fields, outfits the leaves and grass with green and, in so doing, slowly starts to restore the devastation in the hearts of all those who are grieving.

Five (*To Phoebus*) How long does it take for the Sun to cross the sky?

Four Time. A measuring system used to compare the duration of events and intervals between them. Just that? Or is it part of the space-time continuum as often theorised? The motion of planets around the Sun is space-time. So too is the light around a star. In any given space-time, there is absolute uniqueness, independent of any observer.

Two The phases of the moon.

Three The swing of a pendulum.

One The beat of a heart.

Three Each timed and each labelled.

One A second: a specific number of hyperfine transitions in caesium atoms.

Six Time is everything. Time is money.

Five Tears and laughter, birth and death.

Two Time is tearing down and building up.

Three Time is love and hate.

Four   Time started with the act of Creation and ends with the judgement of the Second Coming. Time is war and peace, religion and Theory.

Six   Time is motion.

One   Time is a concept, an illusion. It holds no reality.

Five   Time is waste contemplating the definition of time. We can live in the past going over and over and in the future, hoping and wishing, but where we are now, the present, that's what matters.

Two   There are no answers. We are mere speculators of something... bigger.

One   Time is nature's way of keeping everything from happening at once. Because, even as it is, we sometimes find it hard to cope, to move on, to forgive. And time, certainly, does not heal all wounds.

(*Long pause*)

Two   One pair of eyes

Six   Watches another pair of eyes

Three   That look into another pair of eyes

Four   That are searching in another pair of eyes

One   That look elsewhere, into a pair of eyes

Five   That watch another pair of eyes

Three   That try to get attention from

Two   One pair of eyes

(*Transition. Thisbe is reading Narcissus' palm. Pyramus is close. Echo watches*)

Narc.   So?

Thisbe   Well, you've got a fire hand. And... Ah. It ends here... you're selfish. You should spend more time and energy on who you love.

Narc.   Really?

Thisbe   Ooh.

Narc.   What?

Thisbe   You've got a simian crease.

Narc.   Don't shout. Everyone'll want one.

Thisbe   It's where the heart and head meet.

(*Beat*)

>Single-minded.

Narc. That's ridiculous.

Thisbe Maybe.

Pyra. Where did you learn this?

Thisbe My Mum taught me. Most of it stems from Greek mythology. Each area of the hand relates to a god or goddess. So, for example, the ring finger is Apollo and so everything relates to art, music, aesthetics and so on.

>Want me to do yours?

Pyra. I better not.

Thisbe Sure.

Pyra. If my Dad...

(*Pause*)

Narc. Fear is your enemy. Get a grip.

(*He gives his hand*)

Pyra. Cold hands, warm heart?

Thisbe I love hands. Hands are the eyes to the soul.

(*Pause*)

> A curved line means you are sensitive.
>
> And it ends here... so you are a passionate and emotional person.

Narc. I'm passionate and emotional.

Thisbe We all are.

Pyra. We're all at war.

Narc. What?

(*Beat*)

Pyra. No, just... inside, we're at war with ourselves.

Thisbe Pleasure and Pain.

Pyra. Yes.

(*Beat*)

Narc. 'A plague on both your houses.'

Get a room.

(*He moves away. Pyramus leaves*)

Thisbe (*Looking up*) 'Gallop apace, you fiery-footed steeds, towards Phoebus lodging. Such a waggoner as Phaeton would whip you to the West and bring in cloudy night immediately.'

(*Aglauros appears. Long Pause. Thisbe goes*)

Echo (*Looking up*) A falling star.

Agla. Yes.

(*Beat*)

My brother.

(*Pause*)

Echo I'm sorry about... you know...

Agla. Everyone's sorry.

(*Beat*)

As am I.

Sorry.

(*Pause*)

> Have you seen him?

Echo Who?

Agla. You know who. Pyramus.

> Mum will be in bits if she sees. I wish they got on. Her and his Dad. I don't think they approve of me.

(*Pause. She looks up*)

> I don't see my Dad. Not really.

(*Pause*)

> I think he likes me.

(*Beat*)

> Pyramus.

Echo Really?

Agla. Yes. Why?

Echo No, I just... I thought your sister liked him.

Agla. My sister is misguided.

(*She sees Echo is watching Narcissus*)

As are you.

Echo Why?

Agla. Things... that happen change people. People change.

Echo Who?

Agla. My sister. Him.

Echo Have you changed?

(*Beat*)

Agla. No.

(*Beat*)

Narc. Alright girls?

Agla. Alright?

(*Aglauros nudges Echo to speak*)

Narc. Admiring the view?

Agla. There's not a lot to see.

Echo Shhh. Don't say that.

Narc. Well I'm Ophthalmophobic.

Agla. What's that?

Narc. I don't like being stared at.

Agla. We're only window-shopping.

(*Beat*)

Narc. Yes? Well don't look at what you can't afford.

Agla. No chance. I'm Atelophobic. I don't like imperfection.

(*He moves away*)

Agla. He's so arrogant.

(*Beat*)

You know what they say about him?

Echo What do they say?

Agla. That he cannot, must not, come to know himself.

Echo   What's that supposed to mean?

Agla.   He is the epitome of self-love.

(*Beat*)

    I think he likes me though.

(*Pause*)

Echo   (*Sarcastic*) How are you ever going to choose?

Agla.   I'll have them both.

Echo   Right.

Agla.   What?

Echo   Nothing.

(*Pause*)

    If you could have one wish, just one. What would you wish for?

(*Pause*)

Agla.   Everything.

Echo   But that's…

Agla. What, greedy?

Echo I just don't think getting everything you want means happiness.

Agla. What are you, my nemesis? My divine retribution?

Echo Have you heard of the Midas touch? Where everything you touch turns to gold. He – Midas - made that wish.

Midas Imagine if your wishes came true. You'd be so powerful. Everyone would adore and admire you. You'd be able to tell everyone what to do, how to be, how to dress...

Imagine.

(*He picks up things and they change to gold*)

> The imagination is an extraordinary thing. Enough belief can drag fantasy to reality.
>
> Take... a twig... turns yellow and gleams like a jeweller's bauble.
>
> An apple... it changes... you'd think it had come as a gift from the magical tree.

(*He goes to the water and touches it*)

Midas, beside himself, wild with wishes and fantasies, everything turned to gold.

He wanted to celebrate. So he started to eat... but the food chilled, congealed and turned hard in has hand.

A drink then?

But wine too turned to metal.

There was no food to feed his hunger and no liquid to appease his thirst. But he had a nightmare menu of wealth.

(*To the Gods*) Stop now.

Echo Dad?

Midas No. No. Don't.

(*She runs to him and jumps on him. She freezes. He is distraught*)

Midas No. No. My baby.

(*To the Gods*) I don't want this anymore. Stop it. Whoever did this, stop it.

(*He whispers his secret into his hands and then tries to hide it. Aglauros watches*)

Agla. What you doing?

Midas Nothing.

Agla. (*Playful*) What are you hiding?

Midas Nothing.

Agla. Someone's got a secret.

(*Beat*)

Midas If I tell you…

Agla. Yes?

Midas I'll have to kill you.

Agla. Yes.

(*Beat*)

Midas No I can't.

Agla. Oh come on.

Midas I can't.

Agla. You're no fun.

(*She leaves. He is being watched by Hunger*)

Hung. Hunger had smelt his greed and made its way towards him, finally latching its cadaverous arms around him and breathing its spirit into his lungs, setting his pumping veins into spasms of need and his mouth into a salivating hell, like a cold-turkey addict gone rotten.

(*He tries to remove himself from Hunger*)

Midas Starving. Ravenous.

Hung. He eats and eats and eats… but simply never fills.

Midas It's not enough.

Hung. It's never enough. He cannot be satisfied.

(*He gets more and more desperate*)

Midas I must have more.

Hung. An unfillable black hole of chaos.

Hunger unabated, his fortune swallowed up… In time he had spurned or scared everyone in his life.

Midas   (*To the Gods*) Help me!

(*Pause. He goes to the water and frantically washes*)

    Get rid of it. The guilt. The greed. The hunger.

Hung.   Each thing leeched out into the water. It produced gold and left on its banks nuggets…

    (*At Thisbe*) …of temptation.

Thisbe   Hiya.

(*Pause. Midas sees Thisbe*)

Midas   No. No.

(*Beat. He changes rapidly/ split personality*)

    Come here. Come on. I won't hurt you.

    No, stay where you are.

Thisbe   Why?

Midas   Come to me.

    Stay there.

(*Beat*)

If she stays…

(*Beat*)

You should go now.

Thisbe Why?

Midas Please, just go.

Thisbe Are you sure you're alright?

Midas Go!

Echo Alone and desperate and as much for everyonw else's safety, finally he ate himself. A deplorable act of self-cannibalism.

(*Transition*)

(*Aglauros sees Echo see Pyramus. Narcissus watches*)

Agla. You like him.

Echo No.

Agla. You want him for yourself.

Echo I don't.

Agla. You're the Midas. And I'm your Nemesis.

Eat your own words from now on.

(*With everyone watching Narcissus goes to Echo. He shows sympathy. He playfully tries to look in her eyes. She softens. He touches her. She can't believe it. They look into each others eyes. He kisses her. Pause. Then he spits and retches. Everyone laughs. Echo is in pieces, tears in her eyes. She tries to speak. Cant. She is ridiculed. The more she tries to get words out, the more she is ridiculed*)

Five Narcissism: the libidinal compliment to the egoism of the instinct of self-preservation. Or, simply, the desire and energy that drives our instinct to survive.

(*A fawning group forms around Narcissus*)

> One theory suggests that we are not born with a sense of ourselves, but the ego starts to develop through childhood as the outside world intrudes, teaching us about standards and, therefore, aspirations and expectations within the social environment.
>
> Narcissists cannot see the impact of their actions. They need continuous proof of their worth, their voice.

> Humility is a veil that conceals the features of greatness.

Narc. If only I had a little humility... I'd be perfect.

(*Laughter*)

Five Vanity is a mask that disguises the face of misfortune.

Narc. The only difference between God and I is that God doesn't think he is me.

(*Laughter*)

(*Everyone gathers for a photo to be taken with Narcissus*)

Five So, whilst attracting fawners, fantasists and flatterers to look and value them, hoping for reflected glory and boosting...

Narc. This won't do.

(*He removes someone from the photo*)

Five ...they heartlessly break hearts and spurn friendships.

Narc. (*At someone else*) Look at you. You can't be serious.

Five   If they are not heard the childhood wound opens, finding flaws and criticism in everyone.

Narc.   (*At someone's clothes or hair*) And what's that? It's ridiculous.

Five   People cannot tolerate them for long, so they lead fragmented, often lonely lives.

(*People moving away. He faces one person*)

Five   Even when disaster stares you in the face, there is no doubt and no remorse.

Narc.   It isn't my fault.

(*Alone, he screams after them*)

> It's all of you. You're pathetic. You've got no guts. No zest.

(*Alone, he takes photos of himself. Others watch*)

Two   Love is the blind ignorance of youth.

Three   Love is a blinding fog which prevents the soul from seeing the truth.

(*Narcissus alone. Echo cannot be seen by him*)

Echo   I am fully aware that your greed means you want what you can't get. I want you to want me but I can't be honest and let you know because then you won't want me.

But if I'm dishonest I'll fall apart.

But at least then, you won't be able to get to me, because I won't even know you're there.

Maybe then, you'll love me.

Narc.   Is anyone there?

Echo   One there?

Narc.   Come here.

Echo   Come here.

Narc.   No, you come here.

Echo   You come here.

Narc.   We must come together.

Echo   Together.

(*Echo stands before Narcissus*)

Narc.   Oh its you.

Echo   It's you.

Narc.   (*Defensive*) Yes.

Five   They become mirror images: He ruthlessly selfish, she relentlessly selfless. But both are anxiously attached: she clings insufferably to her object of desire, whilst he keeps his at a distance. The more she's there, the more he needs her to be.

Narc.   I am not in love with this person, but I am in love with the fact that it loves me. It makes me feel good and I love myself more - not it. And yet the more I love myself the more it loves me. No wonder I can't end this ridiculous game. I wouldn't know I loved myself.

Five   They become completely co-dependent and yet are so very, very far apart.

Narc.   Can't keep away?

Echo   Keep away.

Narc.   I'm nowhere near you.

Echo   Near you.

Narc. Wouldn't want to be.

Echo Want to be.

(*Beat*)

Narc. Near you.

Echo You.

(*Beat*)

Narc. Look, pack it in.

Echo Pack it in.

Narc. You pack it in.

Echo You... pack it in.

(*Pause*)

Narc. Oh, I see how this works.

Echo How this works.

(*Beat*)

Narc. You are beautiful.

Echo   You are beautiful.

(*Both smile*)

Narc.   You're gorgeous.

Echo   You're gorgeous.

Narc.   I know.

Echo   I know.

(*Pause. Narcissus' dawning. He stares at Echo*)

Narc.   Inside, you are ugly.

Echo   You are ugly.

(*Pause. He turns away*)

Narc.   I can't help you.

Echo   Help you.

(*Pause. Narcissus breaks down*)

Narc.   Who am I?

Echo   Who am I?

(*Pause. She moves closer*)

Narc. I don't know who I am.

Echo Who. I. Am.

(*Pause. She goes to hold him*)

Narc. What do you think you're doing? I'd rather die than let you touch me.

Echo Touch me.

(*Echo's heart physically breaks. She changes*)

Echo Echo removed herself from everyone and everything.

Narc. Something's missing

Five The ego-libido is directed to the self. Object libido is directed to persons outside ourselves.

Three Echo slowly wasted away until only her voice and bones remained, which then turned to stone.

Narc. I'm changing.

Five When ego and object are converted through the act of giving to another, less ego-libido is then available to protect and nurture the self and therefore, the narcissistic state. If and when the affection is returned, so too is the libido.

Echo Never seen, but often heard, her voice lived on in the sound of the Echo.

Narc. Who's there?

Five But... any failure to achieve, or disruption of, this balance can, through time, cause psychological disturbances.

Narc. What's happening to me?

Two He made me cry so many times.

Narc. Is it raining?

Three He told me he liked some of my qualities but that he had to see other girls.

Six He plays too many games. He doesn't know real friendship.

Narc. I can't tell anymore.

Two If he didn't get what he wanted he'd just start telling me about all the other girls.

Six   I pity him.

Three   I wish he'd suffer.

Two   I wish he'd fall in love...

Three   What?

Two   Deeply, painfully, ridiculously in love. But realise its impossible, because he's unable to have them.

Narc.   (*To the watchers*) I know I'm irresistible but you don't have to stare.

Six   The most incredible moment is when we learn to love and to be loved.

Narc.   (*Shouts*) Hey, where are you?

(*He imitates her*)

>   (*Shouts*) Oi. I know you're out there. Somewhere.

(*He imitates her*)

>   I don't need her. I don't need anyone. Just me.

(*Narcissus is at water*)

>   Just me.

A strange new thirst, an unfamiliar craving enters my body and my eyes. I have never seen such beauty.

(*He goes closer to it. With his eyes. Tries to kiss it. Tries to touch it*)

(*Angry*) Do not mock me.

(*To himself*) Get up. Leave.

(*He stands and starts to move away. Stops*)

I can't. I cannot leave.

(*Shouts*) Who's playing me? Come on. Who's doing this?

(*He returns and stares into the water. Softens*)

I'm deluded. But what love is not delusion?

Our hearts are as one, but our bodies are apart, reaching out across a chasm. You smile when I do, cry when I do, your humour, your grief, your understanding of every thought that crosses my mind. I read those lips and watch them repeat my words… but I can never hear them…

I know you… I know myself.

(*Pause*)

    I am on fire with a love for myself.

Five   He can never really know himself because he cannot see himself as anything other than his own perception.

    Nevertheless...

    Narcissism can develop into a severe personality disorder. The patient may have overestimated his need for affirmation, which has become excessive. It may become impossible for the patient to live a productive or happy life through a complete disregard for feeling and need.

Narc.   It's okay. I have nothing else to give. And I know that you too will make death's sacrifice for me. And we'll be together. Truly together.

(*Pause*)

    You're blurring... my tears... they're rippling the water... I can't see you...

(*He thrusts his hands in*)

    No. Come back.

Narc.   Do not desert me.

Echo   Desert me.

Narc.   Stay, please.

Echo   Please.

Narc.   I love you.

Echo   You.

Narc.   Please stay.

Echo   Stay.

Echo   Consumed by the hidden fire of love, death gently closed the eyes which so admired only their own beauty.

There was no body to be found.

(*She takes a flower*)

Just a flower with white petals round a yellow centre.

And she... she removed herself.

(*Metamorphosis of Echo into Pomona. She starts to paint on a wall*)

Pom. Free from love and all the pain that goes with it, she found a new voice and channelled everything into her art.

(*Aglauros admires herself in the water*)

Agla. I'm changing.

(*Looks around to see if anyone is around*)

I'm changing.

(*Pomona observes the two figures*)

Pom. The Metamorphosis of Narcissus by the surrealist artist, Salvador Dali. This famous painting uses repeated images of similar configuration with interconnected significance. The figure of Narcissus becomes a hand holding a cracked egg from which springs a narcissus flower. The relationship between reality and illusion is perfectly embodied. In the background you can see a small group of expectant heterosexuals.

(*Metamorphosis of Narcissus into Vertumnus, who stares at Pomona*)

Vert. Only when we lose it do we truly know what we want.

Conscience...

(*Out, Loud*) Where are you Nemesis? You restrain the frivolous insolence of mortals and dish out retribution like meals at the last supper.

(*He presents a bravado and a desperation*)

(*To Pomona*) Also in the painting, even though it is spring, is the God of Snow, whose head is leaning over the dizzy space of reflection and beginning to melt with desire.

(*Beat*)

Agla. Unrequited love is the worst love of all. It's like a hole in a sock. Mend it or get rid of it. Don't just stand there with cold feet.

Vert. You like art?

(*Beat*)

I'm an artist.

(*Beat*)

Yes, I love it. I do it. I am it. It is me. It confounds and decimates me. It annihilates me. It fuels me. It...

Pom. We're all artists. In life. All of us.

Vert. Yes. I suppose so.

Pom. We create constantly.

Vert. Yes. I do. Constantly.

Pom. In every thought. In every word. And every time we look into someone's eyes.

Unless they're lying.

(*She leaves. He follows*)

Vert. Yes, I was going to the gallery. The art gallery. Maybe you'd like to come?

(*Transition. Aglauros and Thisbe, watched by Pyramus*)

Agla. If you listen to what you criticise most severely, you'll hear what you most fear you are, won't you?

Thisbe Yes. You have to be who you want to be. Not what everyone else wants.

Agla. Yes, but they don't know what they want.

(*Pause. Long look at Pyramus*)

Thisbe I do.

(*Beat*)

Agla. I'll talk to him.

Thisbe Promise.

Agla. Thisbe, I promise.

Now go.

(*Thisbe leaves*)

Bless her. She hasn't got a clue. Unrequited love is the worst of all.

(*She readies herself as Pyramus appears*)

Agla. Alright?
You're being bold. You'll get in trouble if either of our parents see you.

Pyra. I don't care.

Agla. Oh. Rebellion too. Impressed.

Pyra. I'll take that risk.

(*Pause*)

I am here to ask something… to say something.

Agla. Are you?

Pyra. I am here… for love… for the sake of love. A love that won't go away, that won't be suppressed by discipline or rules. A love that burns as bright as the sun, that makes traffic stop, that brings electricity to a pause, that puts out the lights, that makes the world silent.

If you are true and faithful…

Agla. Yes.

Pyra. If you are true and faithful…

Agla. Come on.

Pyra. In time…

…you will be an adored aunt…

Agla. Aunt?

Pyra. Yes… to our children!

> Me and Thisbe.

Agla. Thisbe?

> Oh right.

(She physically changes. Pyramus doesn't see. A moment magnified)

> She felt her heart break into a thousand pieces, the shards spreading around her body, their sound reverberating through her head. Unrequited love is the hardest thing to bear. The sudden loss of dignity, the hours wasted hoping, believing, the fantasies imagined, the future seen and believed. Fate. Destiny. These words become termites burrowing into the mind.

(Envy/ Lycaon is watching)

Envy/ Lyc. Metamorphoses start somewhere, deep within us, against our will, on a subconscious level. The heart begins to beat, with a new, darker rhythm, like a funeral drum, the march of death, where, spurred on, anything is possible. The hurt twists itself into a clinging root of envy, suffocating the good and breathing new life into the bad.

(*The moment resolves*)

Pyra. Do you know where she's gone?

Agla. No.

Pyra. Oh.

(*Pause. He starts to leave*)

Agla. She doesn't like you.

Pyra. Really?

Agla. No.

Pyra. Has she said that?

Agla. Pretty much.

Pyra. I thought she did.

(*Beat*)

Agla. I could get her to.

Pyra. Could you?

Really?

(*Pause*)

Agla. This is where you ask for my help.

Pyra. Will you?

Agla. Will I what?

Pyra. Help me.

Agla. I might.

What will you give me?

Pyra. Urm…

Agla. Come on. What will I get out of it?

(*She touches him*)

Pyra. You can't mean…

Agla. Can't I?

(*Pause*)

Pyra. That's horrible.

Agla. Don't be so naïve.

Pyra. That's... that's blackmail.

Agla. Meet me later.

No one will know. It'll just be our little secret.

You and me.

(*Pause. He goes*)

Envy She hadn't gone unobserved. Envy was watching.

Envy was a terrible insomniac, completely preoccupied by the triumphs of those detested, the better to gnaw on the bitter marrowbone of spite. Once envy is born as an idea, it grows up quickly, metamorphosing into absolute reality.

The ground perished beneath envy's feet, flowers and trees died as it set its sights on its next victim.

Pyra. Pyramus and Thisbe found each other in the gloom.

Thisbe And their love grew.

Pyra. Two tortured souls, so desperately in love.

Thisbe But they felt as if the whole world was against them.

One   (*Calling*) Thisbe?

Five   (*Calling*) Pyramus!

Pyra.   Especially their parents.

One   An ongoing feud between the two families.

Five   Meant there was no way his son was going to be seen with her.

One   I don't want her to be. She can do much better than him.

Five   Better than him? In your dreams.

One   And I'm your worst nightmare.

(*Beat*)

Five   Where is your husband anyway? Oh yes, he's up in Heaven.

One   Don't.

Five   It's no wonder your boy killed himself.

Pyra.   Dad!

Thisbe   He didn't.

(*Beat*)

Thisbe (*To Five*) Why would you say that?

(*Pause*)

One　　It was an accident.

(*Mum walks away*)

Thisbe　Mum.

　　　　　I miss him too.

Five　　(*Grabbing him*) Get in. I don't want you talking to her.

Pyra.　Get off me.

Five　　You'll do as you're told.

Pyra.　I'll do. Whatever. I. Want. To. Do.

Five　　Don't you dare...

(*He hits him. Pause. Thisbe watches*)

Pyra.　You'll regret this.

(*They go*)

Five   Pyramus. Pyramus.

(*Thisbe alone*)

Thisbe (*Looking up*) I'm sorry. If I could take it back, I would. I'd do anything.

Wherever you are, whatever you're thinking, I am so sorry.

Pyra. But nothing could stop them.

Thisbe The more they were kept apart the more they would be pushed together.

Pyra. Secretly conversing, their fire and anger burned all the more furiously for being covered up.

Agla. And what will love not discover?

In the wall between the two houses there was a crack.

Thisbe I've never noticed that before.

Agla. Maybe it was inflicted as a means to an end.

(*Thisbe alone at the wall*)

Thisbe (*Looking up*) Hey. Have you forgiven me yet? Maybe then I can forgive myself.

(*Pyramus joins Thisbe at the wall. They hold hands through the hole*)

Agla. Watching her sister's relationship secretly develop fuelled envy more and more until it finally arrived at her side.

Envy Envy touches the girl's heart. Thorns start to grow and fill her with deadly spikes. Poison seeps into her bloodstream, its contamination moved along even quicker with images of her sister's secret and tortured love.

(*Pyramus and Thisbe close to the wall. Pyramus hurts as Thisbe speaks*)

Thisbe Do you think this wall is cruel separating us? I suppose we owe it the privilege of bringing our words to our ears. Mustn't be ungrateful.

(*Giggling*) Thank you wall.

(*Pause. She tries to sense him*)

I know who you are.

You are so much of me, that if I don't love you I won't exist. And I'm selfish. I don't want to miss anything.

(*Beat*)

Pyramus?

Pyra. Lend me your dreams. Cover me with the innocence of your sleep and the sunshine of your hope. Light my darkness with fireflies and build me castles in the air to house the summers of our love.

(*Beat*)

Thisbe I love your words.

(*Beat*)

Pyra. Sometimes, the pain of love completely outweighs the joy.

Thisbe Yes. Exquisite pain. I like it.

Pyra. But we've never died of it, have we?

Thisbe No. Not yet.

Pyra. Knowing that, that we survive, that we continue to survive through all this, through our being fragile, we become strong. Pain becomes... belief. Faith.

Thisbe Like life and death, joy and pain can't be separated. They become each other.

Five (*Calling*) Pyramus.

One (*Calling*) Thisbe.

(*Both recoil and squirm at the voices*)

Pyra. I will not die of you.

We've got to leave.

Thisbe What?

Pyra. We've got to get away from here.

Thisbe But they'll find us...

Pyra. Do you trust me?

Thisbe I'm scared.

Pyra. Do you trust me?

Thisbe Yes.

Pyra. I won't let anything happen.

Tonight. Meet me at the graveyard. By the mulberry.

Thisbe You'll be there?

Pyra. Yes. I'll be there. And don't worry. We'll be alright.

I love you.

Five (*Calling*) Pyramus.

Pyra. I love you.

Thisbe I love you. I love you.

Agla. I hate it. I hate it.

Thisbe (*Looking up*) 'Gallop apace, you fiery-footed steeds, towards Phoebus lodging…'

If ever I need you, Dad, it is now.

Mum (*Calling*) Thisbe.

(*She goes*)

Agla. I am wasting away, eaten from the inside out. I am being consumed by jealousy.

I don't want to see anymore.

Please. Please, let me go.

(*Through this, as Envy examines her, she changes*)

Envy Her eyes... cease to see. Her body is stiff... her muscles don't work ...her hands... cold. Her flesh... boneless. Breathe... shallow... laboured. Heartbeat... erratic. Her voice?

(*She tries to speak*)

Ceases to find itself... the clay of her flesh hardens... stained by her mind and soul... black, black as coal.

(*Bells chime*)

(*Thisbe approaches. Lycaon watches unseen*)

Thisbe Pyramus. Pyramus.

It's alright. He said he'd be here. Just wait. Sit and wait.

(*She sits and puts her top down next to her. She starts to sing. Lycaon approaches her*)

Lyc.   I thought I'd find you here.

(*Through this he approaches her as she backs away*)

Thisbe   A wolf was searching for food, when he heard a child crying from a window, so he went and crouched beneath it. And he heard the mother say, 'Stop crying or I'll throw you to the Wolf.' So the wolf waited and waited. That evening he heard the mother say, 'If the naughty wolf comes, he shan't get you. Daddy will kill him.'

(*He picks up her top*)

Lyc.   You can't believe a word people say these days.

Thisbe   Some people tell the truth.

Lyc.   Maybe. But your Daddy's not at home.

(*He sniffs her top*)

   (*Gently*) A wolf, the same wolf, had just eaten a baby, but had got a tiny bone stuck in its throat. So he went to this girl and asked this girl to pull it out. 'I'll make it worth your while,' said the Wolf.

(Pause)

> So, even though she was terrified, the girl put her hand in. And then her head, right in... and she removed the bone.
>
> Please?

(Pause)

> But then the wolf let her leave.

Thisbe What about her reward?

Lyc. She can say she put her head in a wolf's mouth and has lived to tell the tale.

> That, I feel, is more than enough.

(Thisbe backs away. Lycaon sniffs deeply on the top and rubs it on his face. As he senses Pyramus coming he places it down. Pomona is watching. Pyramus arrives, out of breathe. He picks up her top and sees Lycaon)

Pyra. It's my fault.

> It's all my fault. I made you leave, I put you in danger and I wasn't here. I should have been here.

To get closer to you, sometimes we have to get further away.

Our parents will suffer for this.

(*He kills himself. In our version Lycaon handed him a poison. Thisbe comes out*)

Thisbe Pyramus, my Pyramus... what's happened to you? Answer me.
It's Thisbe.

Ah, you did it. You did it for me.

I have to be with you. Only death could part us and only now will join us. And my brother.

Be brave.

(*She kills herself. In our version she kissed him so taking the poison. Lycaon tries to stop her, but she dies. He is distraught and runs off*)

Pom. Their blood tinged the white mulberries of the tree with red. It sunk into the earth and reached the roots, snaking up through the trunk to the fruit. The two bodies were buried together and the tree ever after served as a memorial to their love, producing purple berries from that day on.

(*Pause, as she surveys the scene*)

What's happening to this world?

Everyone's dying and I can but weep for them in solitude. A terrible tragedy takes place in my soul. They die in silence, because humanity has stopped listening. They die by the vipers who have filled the air with poison. They die alone and hungry while many are over-full.

And what can we do?

The tiny shred of feeling that might prompt one person to give just a fragment to another is the only virtue that makes us worthy of the light of the day and the peace of the night.

(*Vertumnus approaches her*)

Vert. Beautiful.

It does you credit.

Art imitates life.

Pom. It can't be imitated. It's impossible. And why try to? I want to reveal it's essence, its spirit, its consciousness. Not just as it is.

(The figures of Pyramus and Thisbe rise and walk away together as:)

> The things I witness, these metamorphoses, are like expressionistic episodes. Exquisite pain that shows itself as a tear in my eye and on my lips as a sigh.

Vert. My wish is that it continues as both a tear and a smile.

Pom. Both?

Vert. Yes. Sometimes wishes can come true.

> A tear keeps purity in my heart, reveals the mysteries of life and with which I share misfortune of broken hearts. And a smile brings me closer to my being and expresses my love for existence.

Pom. You can have one without the other.

Vert. What are you scared of? You don't have to be alone. No one is going to steal your uniqueness.

> There's a man I know. I know him as well as he knows himself. He's a good man, trying to be good. He isn't like other men who fall for everyone they see. And I gather he loves the same things you do...

Pom. Coincidence.

Vert. Maybe... But the same things inspire and affect him.

Pom. Sometimes we have to stop trying so hard.

Vert. Perhaps it's fate?

Pom. Did you hear me?

Vert. Destiny then?

And he's not unattractive.

Is he?

(*Beat*)

Pom. I don't know him.

(*Pause*)

Vert. Orpheus was an artist, like you, a musician. He'd been taught by his father, who, now, was no longer with us. But when he played, it was through the memory, the essence of him. He was able to play and move people. He would touch their hearts and their imaginations. Even nature was softened by his notes. But all the music in the world could not suppress his one true love. And absence truly had made the heart grow.

Eur. You're back.

Orph. I'm back.

Eur. Home.

Orph. Where I belong.

Eur. And how were the adoring fans?

Orph. Sycophantic. Living in a fantasy world. They create what they want to see.

Eur. Don't you need a bit of fantasy from time to time?

Orph. It's not real.

Eur. That's the idea. It helps them. From time to time.

Orph. Temporarily. Everything is so temporary.

(Beat)

I've been all over the world. Seen humanity stretched and tortured, pushed to its limits. Despicable atrocities alongside beauty and goodness that takes your breath away. Kindness and love literally hand in hand with greed and hatred. Moments that...force you to question everything... where you're reeling... but then you focus on the present, on this now, just that... and you have to accept and forgive.

(*Beat*)

And through it all, there was only you. I don't want to leave you anymore. I didn't want to see without you, so I'd close my eyes and imagine you there.

Eur. And every night...

Orph. Wherever I was...

Eur. I'd look up...

Orph. And there you were.

Eur. And there I was.

Orph. In the stars.

Eur. On cloud street.

(*Long pause*)

I remember the first time I heard you play...

Do you remember?

Orph. Don't look back.

(*Lycaon and figures appear behind Eurydice. Orpheus sees them*)

Eur. Orpheus?

Orph. Don't look back.

Eur. Why?

Orph. Just focus on me. Come on.

Eur. What's there?

Orph. Leave her alone.

Eur. (*Turns*) What's there?

Orph. Eurydice.

(*Eurydice looks back and she is snapped up by Lycaon and other figures*)

Orph. Eurydice.

(*Screams*) No. No. Don't leave me.

Don't leave me.

(*Pause*)

Give her back. Do you hear me? Give her back.

I know you. I know who you are.

(*Figures gather. The Sound of Hell*)

This isn't real. This isn't real.

(*He looks about him and realises what he must do*)

Okay...

This darkness is the limit of what art can attain and Eurydice the point to which death and night leads. That was the instant night approaches Death. And I must bring it back into daylight to give it reality and form.

Hades? Who enriches himself with our sighs and tears. Notorious, well-guessing Hades, who receives many. I know you won't show yourself.

And Persephone? Abducted and dragged down here. Tricked into staying when he chooses. The flowers you were picking died and there was famine.

(*Silence*)

> Well, I am here. In the prison of the damned souls. There were no rivers of sorrow or hate to cross, no ferryman to pay.
>
> But I am here. An orphic believer.

Four   Your desire is misplaced. Drawn from light to dark, its absence is a mere gap, a notion.

Orph.   No. I am the son of Earth and Starry Heaven. I am thirsty. I drink not from the fountain of forgetfulness, but from the pool of memory. I am redeemed.

(*Silence*)

> Deities of the Underworld, hear my words. They are the truth.
>
> My orphic belief is unfounded but, believe me, I do not come for the secrets of the pit of Tarturus. I do not come to question Thanatos, death, mortality, darkness. Nor his twin Hypnos, sleep. Nor do I come to fight with his offspring, Nemesis, Moros, Momos...
>
> I come for love.

I come for my wife, whose years came to an end...
by a snake... a serpent.

(*Laughter*)

You can't take whatever you want. I want her back.

One You didn't demand by day. But when it is dark, when she is strange to you, then you choose to stake your claim.

Orph. I see her when she is weak, when she is vulnerable. I see her when she despises me. Love has led me here. You know love. You loved enough to steal.

Six Do not compare us.

Orph. She was everything I wanted in a woman. I implore you, by these realms of silence, by these abodes of the unknown, unite again the thread of her life.

I know that we are all destined to you. More than anyone I am resigned to the grievous cycle, to the transmigration of souls, that we are divine, immortal and doomed.

But not her. Not yet. She has so much more to give. Please, not yet.

If I can't take her, then I'll stay and you can have us both.

(*Pause*)

One   The shadows were wet with tears.

Three   The great wheel stopped turning and stood in wonder.

Four   The vultures ceased to gnaw and settled to roost.

Six   You have moved us Orphic.

Three   Time's portion does indeed depend on us...

Four   Absence lengthening...

Three   Presence ending.

One   Perpetual sleep, in time, bursts the vivid folds, whispering to the mind through sweet silence.

Six   But common to all, for nought escapes the all-destructive rage.

Four   You may take her.

Three   But... a scene you will recognise may well be replayed.

Six   One condition.

Do not turn to look at her until you reach real air. Or she will be taken again.

One   And you will lose her for a second time.

Three   Prove your love is real

Four   Do you understand?

Six   Do not look back.

(Image as before. Eurydice behind Orpheus. As she falls he turns and she is taken. Image repeats. Image repeats over and over, slightly different each time. The last time Orpheus tries to chase her, but is stopped)

Eur.   *(During this)* Why did you turn back?
Why did you glance back?
What did you see?
Why did you hesitate?
What crossed my face?
What did you see?

You swept me back. I who have walked with the live souls above and slept with the flowers below, lived unconscious, was almost forgot. If you had let me wait I'd have found peace. If you had let me rest I might have forgotten you and the past. But, for your big moment, I have lost the live souls, the flowers and I have lost you. You who passed across the light, who has his own light, for your arrogance and ruthlessness, I am swept back, broken.

Why? Why did you look back?

Four Grief was multiplied, bruise upon bruise. Cadaverous and stunned, he shut down.

Dwelling obsessively on his past, over and over, his complaints sang to everyone, melting hearts and moving nature, drawing it towards him.

(*People slowly gather*)

One Orpheus?

Orph. Leave me be.

Three Orpheus, please.

Orph. I no longer wish to even look upon another woman.

(*Pause*)

Eur. Orpheus.

Orph. Get away from me.

(*He sees her*)

> Eurydice. Are you real?

Eur. You're forgiven. You must let me go.

Orph. But I failed you.

Eur. There is no failure in loving me too much.

> Don't look back.

> Meet me in the stars, on cloud street.

(*He watches her go*)

One Letting his love and his past go, allowed him to be present.

Three The trees assembled and nodded their leafy heads.

One Animals and beasts came together to hear these things that would expose and soften the pains of the world.

Orph. I will tell you what you already know in your hearts: the pity and the secret of bearing. It can enter you like an ecstatic virus. Ecstasy is to stand outside the self. Nothing must be rejected.

We try to live in a non-reality, fantasy. When we struggle against our energy we reject our wisdom. Anger. Pride. Passion. Grasping at things without thought. We panic, taken over by an emptiness that pervades everything. But it's not real. It's a mirage of desire for the forbidden. And once it's been had, it's unwanted.

We must relinquish opinion and be open and empty of self-attachment. Fearless, brave and above the enemy, beyond the survival of the this, that and I – what is I? – we are destined to burst into an openness that is far more powerful than our wildest dreams.

Pygmalion was an artist, a sculptor. He saw all the heartache in the world and had felt more than his share. So he resolved to live alone, with his work...

Pygm. ...the work of nature.

Some believe that art is the imitation of nature but nature cannot be imitated. Better surely, to communicate something other.

(*He undresses a plastic doll through this*)

Life is raw. Naked. And a naked body surely represents the finest symbol of it. It is vulnerable, beautiful to touch, to look at. A mountain of human shapes shows the mountain is a mass of living things. A waterfall of naked bodies shows a rushing stream of life.

Four   Extraordinary.

Pygm.   Thank you.

Four   Whether he set out to or not, consciously or not, he had created his perfect woman. Perhaps the perfect woman.

(*He sets his statue/ Alcyone*)

Pygm.   She is exquisite. I know she is not real but...she is perfect. She is everything I want in a woman.

(*Through this a physical sequence of Man and Doll/ Statue*)

Four   But no matter what one chooses to call it...

Pygm.   I choose to call it Art.

Four   ...no matter what it is made of, whether marble, wax, plastic, rubber... and no matter what one's feelings and desires are towards one's new ...friend... it all adds up to the same thing. Agalmatophilia: attraction and desire to a doll, statue, mannequin or robot.

This can vary... from actual contact with said object, a fantasy of with animate or inanimate object or objects, of watching perhaps one object with another object, or even the idea of changing, of metamorphosing into an object oneself. Whichever is ones chosen... preferred... outlet, the fantasy aspect is paramount.

But who are we to judge? We are living in an increasingly alarming virtual world, that is predominantly based on pretence and this is a blossoming subculture of luring sirens, inanimate co-conspirators, speechless vessels, where the cusps between art and fantasy blur like faded watercolours. Because here is a woman who appears to be perfect.

She does whatever he chooses without question. Eager to please, she never lies, cheats, is completely accepting of any whim or desire, regardless of what or how often it may be required. She never says No and she never gets pregnant. She wears exactly what he wants her to wear. She is loving and sensitive, a gentle courtesan offering companionship and solace... a great listener... She speaks only when spoken to, or when he imagines she does. When he whispers in her ear that she is his...

Pygm. One and only.

Four   He can almost hear the murmur that the feeling is mutual.

(*Pygmalion stops and takes her in*)

Pygm. This is crazy.

    I can't hear the murmur.

    I know… I know she is not real. And I know that I am alone. Sad, desperate and alone.

(*Pause*)

    Help me, you Gods. Help me.

    Let me feel again. Feel real love again.

    Let me love. Let me love as I love her.

(*He is broken. Pomona watches*)

Pom. This moment.

(*To Lycaon*)

    At his most vulnerable, he is truthful and honest.

    And only then can she return.

(*He assumes there is no change so he goes to her to say goodbye. He passionately kisses her. He notices a change. He kisses her again. She delicately starts to move. He touches her. Feels her body*)

Pygm. Thank you.

(*She looks at him and smiles. They come together*)

Orph. The fantasy became reality. Relinquished. Open and empty.

It's this now that matters. Only the present. And it's exquisite pain.

Lyc. Enough. I don't want to hear anymore.

It is your turn, Orphic.

Orph. It doesn't matter.

Only the present.

(*Lycaon kills Orpheus. In our version he strangled him*)

Lyc. Through those lips to which rocks had listened, which wild beasts had adored and understood, his last breath slipped away and vanished in the wind, like an Echo…

(*He looks around and then at Pygmalion*)

What happens next?

Pygm. (*Eyeballing Lycaon*) A beast was still eager to kill and maim the essence of love.

Lyc. I'm just the messenger.

Pygm. It needed to be stopped, once and for all.

Alcy. Please don't. I have had visions. Dreams, terrible dreams.

Pygm. I must. This is not a mere wolf. It is a monster. The earth is littered with mauled carcasses, mutilated emotions and broken hearts. And still it's there.

Alcy. I am begging you.

Pygm. Nothing must stop our love growing when we've only just begun.

Trust me.

Alcy. How can you leave me alone? Everyone I have ever loved as left me.

Pygm. Don't say that.

Alcy. I'm not blaming you. I'm not. But I'm so scared. If you die, my life is over. Either way, I shall be cursed with every breath as I wait for your return.

Pygm. And I will return. Until then, you must be brave.

(*They hold each other. He finally pulls away from her*)

Alcy. With tears in her eyes she stared out at the man with whom she shared all the love in the world, simply walk away.

(*She looks up and around for answers*)

> A piece of her was missing. A husk remained, a derelict something that she didn't even recognise.

(*She starts to pray*)

(*Lycaon and Pygmalion face to face. A battle of love and hate*)

Pygm. He thinks of his wife… but nothing comes.

(*Lycaon starts to laugh*)

> He is silent, dumbstruck.

(*He finds strength and eyeballs Lycaon*)

> He envies all those men who were at home.

(*Lycaon stops laughing*)

>He thinks of his wife who begged him not to leave.

Lyc. No, no...

Pygm. He calls to the gods... Mercy. Mercy.

Lyc. (*Recoiling in pain*) No.

Pygm. And he calls to his wife, again and again.

>(*Screams*) Alcyone. Alcyone.

(*Lycaons agony increases as the cries come. The prayer increases in volume and intensity, the noise growing, until Hypnos and Morpheus appear. Lycaon and Pygmalion slowly freeze*)

One And then there was silence and stillness.

Two (*At Alcyone*) The prayers, the waiting, meant nothing. But that she loved.

>(*To Hypnos*) Perhaps too much?

One Perhaps.

(*Through this the prayer dries into sleep*)

So, Hypnos, Sleep, crept from her space, where soporific blossoms and narcoleptic odours nod into oppressive air, where fragments of ill-assorted dreams hover and float with the currents, falling into sumptuous billows, where a total silence just allows the sound of breathe. A painted stillness.

She fluttered her heavy eyelids and....

(*She falls asleep*)

Two It is said that prayers for the lifeless create exhaustion in the skies. So Iris, the rainbow, spread a thousand colours through the air, like the most exquisite painting, an expressionistic dream.

The colours awoke the cloud-wrapped twilight.

(*Pause*)

(*Loud*) Somnolent one...

(*She wakes*)

...soother of souls and healer of pained bodies and minds...

(*Surveys the scene*)

One Yes. Now. Which of the children to use? Retribution? Suffering? Doom? Deception? Blame?...

Two You forgot Old Age.

One Yes.

Two What about your brother?

One Thanatos? You mean just kill her?

(*Beat*)

Where is he anyway?

(*Surveys the scene*)

Two Clearly, not far.

One I think he's bored.

Two You forgot me!

One Which one are you?

Two Morpheus, Creator of Dreams.

Hypnos had summoned one of his children, Morpheus, the creator of Dreams, who knew the secret of human form and could look and sound like anyone.

One   Together they devised a form to resemble her lost love and release her from her agony.

Two   Stop yawning.

On noiseless wings, Morpheus darted through the air…

(*Morpheus goes to Pygmalion*)

And slowly took on his human form.

(*Pygmalion appears to Alcyone*)

Alcy.   I'm not scared.

Pygm.   Do you not know me? Look upon your husband's ghost.

Alcy.   I told you. I begged you not to go.

Pygm.   Get up from your bed.

Alcy.   Yes. We should be together.

Pygm.   Beyond death the body is beyond harm. The soul survives and moves on, taking on new form.

Alcy. Yes.

Pygm. Do not allow my shadow to go unlamented.

Alcy. He's gone. And I am gone.

(*Pause*)

Pom. And they both slowly became birds, kingfishers.

Together they fly just over the waters surface and each year Alcyone and her love charm the elements to give way to halcyon days, where tranquillity and hope sit in the clouds, hand in hand with their feet up.

(*Pause*)

Vert. Orpheus was buried and birds would sing beautifully over his grave. He passed once more into the underworld, where he and Eurydice found each other.

They walk together now, taking it in turns to walk in front.

And he looks at her whenever he chooses.

(*Pause. Vertumnus and Pomona looking at each other*)

Relinquished.

There is no I. There is no panic. No need or want.

Open and empty.

(*Pause*)

Pom. This moment is like the sun bursting through a cloud.

Vert. I could say so much more.

Pom. Don't. I have everything I need.

(*Pause*)

The greatest gift by far is to learn to love and be loved.

Alcy. We will ascend to the heavens.

Eur. And, whether child or parent, man or woman…

Orph. Reign as a figure of selflessness and empathy, in the present, just as in the past and the future.

Pygm. Our words will continue, will live on regardless, ascending as high as the sky…

Vert. And among the stars our names will never die...

Pom. But twinkle on forever, becoming one and living, with Hope.

The End